I0016344

Windows 10 in Use

William Rowley

Copyright © 2015 by William Rowley.

All rights reserved. No part of this publication may be reproduced, distributed, or transmitted in any form or by any means, including photocopying, recording, or other electronic or mechanical methods, without the prior written permission of the author, except in the case of brief quotations embodied in critical reviews and certain other noncommercial uses permitted by copyright law.

Table of content

Introduction

Most of you are waiting for the official release of Windows 10. This Operating System (OS) will come in various versions. Windows phones and tablets will be able to support this operating system. The same case applies to Intel-based PCs and laptops. However, the OS comes with advancements and as well as new features for the computing world. These changes range from the time of logging into the system up to when using the system. You should know how to use this OS.

Chapter 1: Definition of Windows 10

Windows 10 is a computer operating system developed by Microsoft, and it belongs to the Windows NT family of computer operating systems. The operating system was released on June, 29 2015. After Windows 8 was released, Microsoft noticed that it received a very poor reception in the market. This is why they saw the importance of developing Windows 10 so as to cover the deficiencies.

According to the definition by Microsoft, the operating system will be supported on computers, phones and tablets. The main advancement introduced in this operating system is that it will be cloud-based. Most of the components for both the cloud and local versions of the OS will be updated on a regular basis. This means that you will always be using the advanced and latest features of the OS.

Once the OS is released, Microsoft made it clear that the users of Windows 8.1, Windows 7, and Windows Phone 8.1 will get an upgrade to Windows 10 for free. Currently, the price of this operating system for other users has not been made clear. Currently, Windows 10 is under test and most users have it installed in their machines. This version runs on Intel-based laptops, PCs, and other hybrid devices.

Windows 10 mobile was made available on February 2015 but it is in test form. Note that this version can only run on Windows based phones and tablets. Devices such as ATMs, kiosks, and point-of-sale terminals will use Windows 10 "Industry" SKU. Windows 10 server will also be available, and it will be used in server computers in production environments. This shows how diverse the operating system is offering satisfaction to the users.

Chapter 2: Minimum Hardware Requirements for Windows 10

Microsoft stated that the PC version of Windows 10 will be released with the same specification as Windows 7 and Windows 8.1. However, more details about the same have been provided. The OS will need a screen resolution of a minimum of 800 * 600. The Pro version of the OS will require a display size of at least 7 inches, while the consumer variants of the operating system will require a display size of at least 8 inches.

The 32-bit version of the operating system will require PCs with at least 1GB of RAM and 16GB of disk space. For the 64-bit version of the OS, the device should have a minimum of 2GB RAM and 20GB disk space.

For new PCs, the following are the requirements:
Firmware- UEFI 2.3.1 with the Secure Boot enabled.
TPM- this is optional, and it can be TPM 1.2 or 2.0.
RAM- 1 GB (32-bit) or 2GB (64-bit).
Storage- 16 GB (32-bit) or 20 GB (64-bit).
Screen- 7-inches or larger (Professional) or 8-inches or larger (consumer), 800 x 600 resolution and above.
Graphics- DirectX 9.

Hardware buttons for a tablet. Start and rotation lock are optional.

Audio- this is optional.

Wireless- this is optional.

Cellular radio- this is optional, can be only data or data and voice.

Sensors- this is optional.

Notification (vibration) - this is optional.

Touch- this feature is optional, and if present, it should be at least two-finger touch.

In the case of phones, the RAM should have at least 512MB while available space should be at least 4GB. This can be provided via the micro SD card which allow for updates of the OS. However, the good thing with it is that most Windows phones usually come with a memory of 8GB which is built-in. The screen size should be between 3 to 7.99 inches. This shows that the version of this OS for phones can be used to power some tablets.

The required resolution will be determined by the amount of RAM that the device has. If the device has a RAM of 512MB, then it must have a minimum resolution of 800 x 480 pixels, while those with a RAM of 4GB should have a minimum resolution of 2560 x 2048 pixels.

Chapter 3: Logging in to Windows 10

It is easy for one to get stuck after starting their computer using Windows 10. This is because the login screen doesn't come up directly as in the previous versions of the Windows OS such as Windows 7.

Once you boot up your computer, you will be presented with a startup screen. This is shown below:

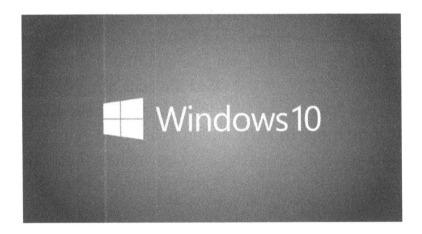

If you are used to other versions of Windows, such as Windows 7, then you will be stuck since you will not be directly taken to the login screen. To get to this, just click on the above screen with your mouse or click the "Up" arrow key. This will take you to the login screen.

It is in the login screen where you can provide your password. Before logging in to the system, just look at the bottom right of the login screen. There will be three options.

The three options will allow you to either sleep, shutdown, or restart the PC. There are two buttons at the bottom left of this screen. These are for Internet Connectivity and Ease of Access.

Just type your password, and click the "->" arrow or press the "Enter" key. This will get you to the home screen of your computer.

You will have successfully logged in. In case the password that you provided is wrong, then you will remain in the login screen.

Chapter 4: File Explorer in Windows 10

When you install Windows 10 in your computer and then you log in, you will be stuck on how to access your files. Suppose you want to get to the Local Disk C, how do you go about it? This is a problem to new users of this operating system.

However, Windows 10 comes with a file explorer icon pinned at the bottom of the home screen. This is shown in the figure below:

You know what happens when you click on the "Start" button? You will be presented with a window with many icons which not take you to your files. Just click on the file explorer icon shown in the above figure. This will take you to folders which are frequently accessed on your system. These can be the following:
Desktop
Videos
Downloads
Music
Documents

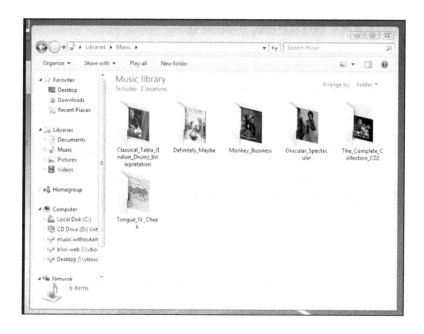

Once you get to the above window, you can navigate to any directory that you want on your computer. This will be just by clicking using the mouse.

Chapter 5: Windows store

In Windows 10, you can directly access the Windows store just from the taskbar available at the home screen of your machine. See the figure shown below:

It is also possible to access from the start menu. Just click on the start button on the home screen of your computer, or press the start key on your keyboard.

You will get to the following window:

The arrow shown in the above figure shows the icon for the store. Just click on the icon, and you will get to the Windows store. It will be in a boxed window, as shown in the following figure:

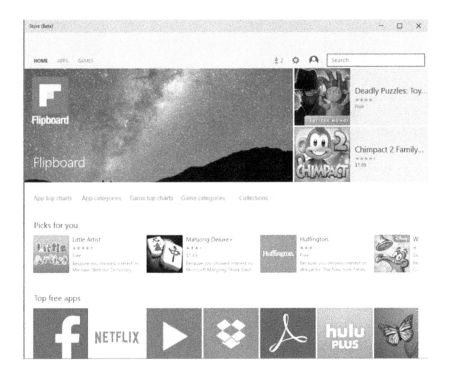

If you click on the app categories, a menu will be opened, and you will be in a position to refine your selection. You can choose to sort using the following means:

Top grossing

Top free apps

Best rated apps

Top paid apps

You will also find a new category called "New and rising."

Chapter 6: The keyboard

Once you are at the home screen of your computer running Windows 10, you can access the keyboard by clicking on the following icon:

The icon is located at the bottom right of the screen. Just click on it, and observe what will happen. The keyboard will pop up as shown below:

The keyboard is the same as what you had in Windows 8.1.

Chapter 7: The Task view in Windows 10

This feature is useful when you are carrying out multiple tasks and you want to distribute them across multiple screens. If you are working on different projects, each of these projects can be run on its own desktop. To switch from one task to another, you only need to change your desktop. To return to the previous task, you just go back to its window. The task you were working on will be there just waiting for you.

To access the task view, you can click on its icon, which is located at the bottom of the screen. This is shown below:

Just click on the icon, and observe what will happen. A hover bar will be shown having a plus sign and a text labeled "Add a desktop."

Just click on it. You will add a new desktop on which you can perform some extra tasks. The task doesn't have to be related to what you were doing in the previous window.

Chapter 8: Notifications

You can access notifications by clicking on a button located at the bottom right of the screen. This is shown below:

A section will be opened at the right part of the screen, and it will show the following set of options:

Connect
Display
All Settings
Tablet Mode

If you need to expand it, click on the link labeled "Expand." After the expansion, the following options will appear:

Rotation Lock
Wifi
Location
VPN

Chapter 9: Backup in Windows 10

For those of you who have used Windows 8.1, you must have the "File History Option" which allows you to back up your files in Libraries, desktop, contacts, and favorites. This was automatically done for you after turning on the opening screen, and then choosing where the files should be backed up.

In Windows 10, this feature has been given a new name, that is, Backup — pun intended. It is also possible for you to configure the backup property so that it can backup certain locations for you and not to backup others. In Windows 10, this setting can be controlled in the Settings application. It can be turned either on or off, select the drive where the drive is to be made, and perform the backup manually.

First of all, define the location of the backup.

Go to the option, and then select "Add a Backup Location." During this, you are advised to select and use an external drive for this purpose. If a network location is important, then you have the choice of selecting it. After everything is set up, a screen will be shown telling you how much space the backed up data has taken.

The drive will also be shown, as well as the last date when you performed a backup of your files.

Chapter 10: Recovery in Windows 10

In the Settings option, you will also find a choice where you can recover your files. The settings in this case are also very simple. The only difference is that in this case, you find some extra options. These are for assisting you in case something goes wrong.

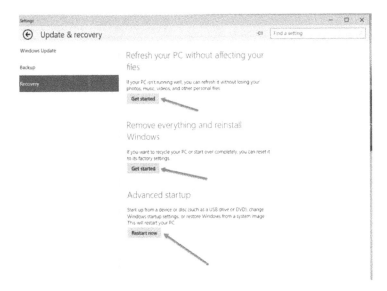

Let us discuss the functionalities offered by these options:

Refresh your PC without affecting your files- this is like a push rest button just as the name suggests. In case your computer develops an issue related to performance, this will help you in uninstalling the window, but it reinstalls it afresh.

This is very important because you will not need to look for installation media, setting up discs and USB drives. The good thing with this is that a very short period of time will be taken compared to the other previous versions of the OS.

All the data that you had saved in your computer, all the applications that you had installed, and the settings which you had applied will all be retained after this process.

Chapter 11: Touchscreen Desktop

The Windows 10 desktop works very well with the mouse and the keyboard. It is made up of tiny bars and thin buttons. This will not be supported in Windows 10. In case you are using the desktop on your tablet which supports touchscreen, then consider buying a portable mouse and keyboard.

If you need to tap on the start menu, then the figures will be good for doing this. However, there are touchscreen controls which are present on the desktop. The following pointers will help you on how to use your fingers so as to control the desktop:

Select- To select something on the desktop, then it is good to use your fingertip. In most people, the pad of their fingers is too large, except for those having small hands.

Double-click- this can easily be done using fingertips. If you need to double-click on something which is located on the desktop, then tap it twice.

Right-click- doing this is a bit complex. If you want to right click on an item, then tap on it, but do this gently. A small square will appear onscreen. This option will stay there. You can then choose the option that you need, and the pop up will disappear.

If your device which is running Windows 10 supports a touchscreen, then it is good for you to look for a small Bluetooth mouse and keyboard, and then use them to operate it. It becomes difficult for you to navigate via touch on small devices.

Chapter 12: Changing Resolution of the Display

Once you change the resolution of your display device, may it be a monitor, a projector, or any other kind of display device; you will notice a change in the size of the elements which are displayed, such as folders and icons. If you use a higher resolution, then these elements will look small.

The effect of resolution on the size of icons is indirect. Note that each character of text and each icon is defined as a number of pixels at a certain resolution. Example, an icon might consist of 36 pixels. However, this icon will be displayed differently on different monitors. This depends on the size of the display, may it be the display of a PC, a tablet, or a phone. Note that the sharper the display, the higher the price. If the screen is of high resolution, then it will be a problem for you to see tiny icons and text.

To change the resolution of your display, follow the procedure below:

At the home screen of Windows 10, just right click and then choose "Display Settings." This will open up the settings application.

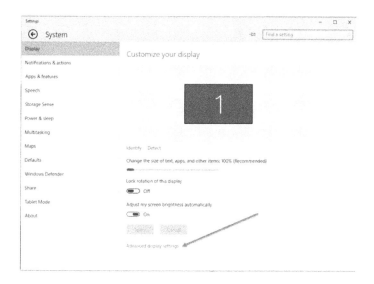

You will be taken to the display settings as shown in the above figure. Choose "Advanced Display Settings" as shown in the above figure. You will be taken to a window with various resolution settings. The resolution will depend on the display monitor and the display adapter. This means that all settings will not be displayed at once.

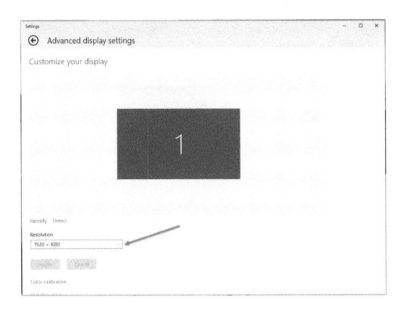

You can then choose the best resolution for your device. Once selected, choose "Apply," and then click on "Keep changes" after the message has appeared.

Note that decreasing the resolution may cause the resolution to appear a bit fuzzy. Also, if the resolution that you choose has a different aspect ratio compared to the one of your machines, the elements onscreen such as text and icons will appear as if they are squashed or stretched.

Chapter 13: WinX Menu in Windows 10

The Classic Stat Menu used in Windows 8 and Windows 8.1 is not available in Windows 10. Currently, the emphasis is on a bold new Start Screen.

This feature was available in the previous versions of Windows, and it allows the OS users to easily and quickly access tools such as the command prompt, control panel, computer management, task manager, and Run Window.

In Windows 8 and 8.1, these were greatly improved since options for both shutting down and restarting the devices and computer were made available. These were not changed in Windows 10.

Programs and Features
Power Options
Event Viewer
System
Device Manager
Network Connections
Disk Management
Computer Management
Command Prompt
Command Prompt (Admin)

Task Manager
Control Panel
File Explorer
Search

If you need to access this menu easily, just press the Winkey + X on your keyboard. Winkey is the key on the keyboard of your device having the Windows logo. This will quickly bring up the hidden menu. If you want to use the mouse so as to bring up this menu, just point at the start button and right click on it.

The menu will appear. You can then select the option that you need, and then click on it. You will also notice that the options provided are 18 in total. However, these options might increase once Windows 10 is officially released to the market.

Chapter 14: Accessing the Task Manager

With the task manager in Windows 10, you can monitor the performance of your system and then control it. The processes, services, and programs which are running on your computer can be monitored in real time with the task manager.

In case you have opened either Microsoft PowerPoint or Microsoft Word on your system, just open the task manager, and you find them running there together with the resources such as memory that they are using. In case a program such as the Media Player or Microsoft Word stops responding, you can find it in the task manager, and then you can cancel it from running.

There are numerous ways that we can open the Task Manager in Windows 10. These include the following:

Pressing CTRL+ALT+ DEL and then choosing the Task Manager. Note that the keys should be pressed simultaneously.

Pressing CTRL+ SHIFT+ ESC at once.

Pulling the Power users Menu by pressing Win+ X and then choosing "Task Manager."

Right clicking the task bar and then choosing the Task Manager.

By opening Cortana and then typing "Task Manager." You will be presented with a set of options. Just choose "Task Manager."

By typing "Task Manager" while on the start screen. A set of options will appear. Just choose "Task Manager."

If you are logged in as a normal user, you will be prompted by UAC. Just press on the "Yes" button, and you will be allowed to continue. If you are logged in as the administrator, you will not be prompted by UAC.

Chapter 15: Creating a USB Recovery Drive

With a USB recovery drive, it will be possible to boot into advanced start-up options if your Windows fails or stops to boot. It also lets you troubleshoot your system in case this problem occurs. In Windows 10, there is an in-built recovery tool that will let you create a USB recovery drive for your system.

However, you need to be aware that your USB drive will be formatted, losing all the data that it contained. Due to this, it is recommended that you back up all of your data in a separate drive or you use a blank USB drive. This will prevent the loss of data.

The following is the procedure for creating a USB recovery drive:

Open the search box and then type "recovery" in it. A list with the available settings will be presented. Choose "Create a Recovery Drive." You can also:

Open the "Control Panel" and then select "Recovery" from the available options. Click on "Create Recovery Drive."

It is possible for to be prompted to allow the program to make changes to your computer. Just click "Yes" if this is the case. If not, just continue.

Click on the "Next" button so as to continue.

You should have inserted the USB drive by now. If that is not the case, you will be prompted to do so.

Choose the drive that you intend to use. Click on the button labeled "Next," so as to proceed.

The process will continue, and finally it will be over. Your recovery disk will be over.

Chapter 16: Booting into Advanced Startup Options

Advanced Startup Options offers powerful features which can be used for troubleshooting the system in case something goes wrong. These features and tools can also be used to change how the Windows behaves as it starts up. A good example is when you want to boot into safe mode.

With Windows 10, it is easy for the OS user to boot into Advanced Startup mode. To do this, do the following:

Click on the "Start" menu, and then click on "Shutdown." Press the "Shift" key on your keyboard, and then hold it down. Without releasing it, just click on the option labeled "Restart."

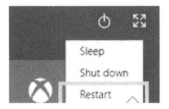

Your Windows 10 will then boot into the Advanced Startup Options. This is just one of the ways we can boot into Advanced Startup Options. It is possible for us to achieve this using the USB recovery drive which we recently created.

Boot the computer by use of the USB recovery drive, and then select the language of your keyboard.

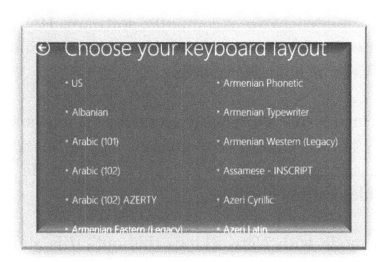

From the "Settings" app, it is possible for you to reboot the computer into the Advanced Startup Options. Just follow the following procedure:

Open "Settings," and then click on the "Update & Recovery" icon. On the left side, you will see an option labeled "Recovery." Just click on this option. Under the "Advanced Startup," you will find an option labeled "Restart Now." Just click on it. Your computer will shut down, and then start in the Advanced Startup Options.

Chapter 17: Starting Windows 10 in Safe Mode

In safe mode, only a few of the Windows components are started. This makes it easy for you to solve any issues related to your computer software. However, you need to know the safe mode options in Windows 10. These include the following:

Safe mode- this is the basic mode for Windows. Only a few of the Windows components run in this mode, and users usually log into this mode for troubleshooting purpose.

Safe mode with Networking- this option is suitable for those who want to access either the network connected to their computer or the Internet. After accessing the Internet while in this mode, you can safely download software, drivers, and browse to the links of your choice.

Safe mode with command prompt- once you boot into this mode, you will not be able to access Windows, but only the command prompt. If you are a novice computer user, then avoid this mode. However, for expert IT Engineers, then this mode is suitable for you.

To boot into safe mode using Advanced Startup Options, follow the procedure below:

Boot into the Advanced Startup Options. If you have forgotten how to do this, consult our previous tutorials.

Find the "troubleshoot" option, and then click on it.

Choose the "Advanced Options" option.

Click on the "Startup Settings."

Choose "restart."

Your computer will then restart. Press the following keys for the various options:

Enter – boot into Normal Mode.

4 or F4 – boot into Safe Mode.

5 of F5 – boot into Sake Mode with Networking.

6 or F6 – boot into Safe Mode with Command Prompt.

To boot into Safe Mode using System Configuration, follow the steps given below:

Open the Run dialog box by pressing windows + R keys on your keyboard.

On the dialog box, type "misconfig," and then click on the "ok" button.

A system configuration window will appear. Click on the tab labeled "boot."

Next to the Safe Mode, you will find a box. Your aim is to boot into one of the three modes. These include normal and the two networking modes. Just choose from the following options depending on what you want:

Minimal- boot into normal Safe Mode.

Alternate Shell- boot into Safe Mode with command prompt.

Networking- boot into Safe Mode with networking.
In the resulting dialog, click on the button labeled "Restart." This will boot your computer into Safe Mode by restarting it.

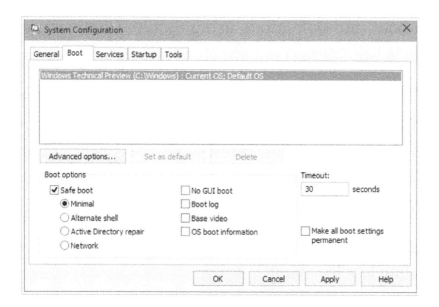

Chapter 18: Disk Cleanup

It is good for you to keep your computer fine-tuned so that you get the best performance from it. Disk cleanup is one of the apps that can help you to maintain your computer.

Disk cleanup works by deleting or cleaning up all the files that you do not want, such as the recycle bin, temporary files, windows old files, system files, and others. Your system will then be in a position to run faster.

Other than using Disk cleanup to clear unwanted files, it can also be used for compression of files in your computer so that you can create additional space on your system. What it does is that it compresses old files and those which have not been opened for a long period of time. This means that there will be creation of additional space on your hard drive. However, you need to note that once a file has been compressed, it will take a longer time to access it compared to accessing a file which has not been compressed.

To open the Disk cleanup app, follow the steps below:

Type "cleanmgr" in the search box of your computer. A number of options will be presented to you. Choose the "cleanmrg" Windows application option.

If you have a single drive on your system, then the better. However, if your system has more than one drives, then select the appropriate one to be cleaned.

You can then select the files which should be cleaned. After the selection, click on the "Ok" button.

A dialog will appear asking you for confirmation. Click on the "Delete files" option.

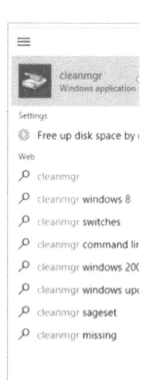

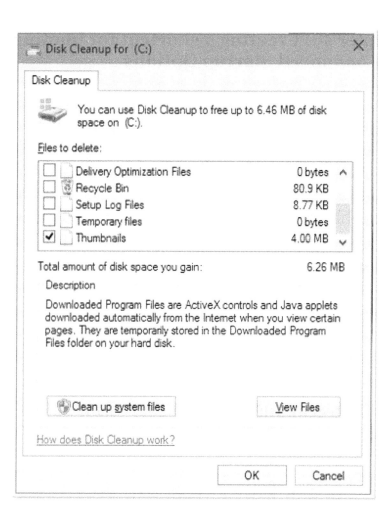

Disk Cleanup for (C:)

Disk Cleanup

You can use Disk Cleanup to free up to 6.46 MB of disk space on (C:).

Files to delete:

☐ Delivery Optimization Files	0 bytes	⌃
☐ Recycle Bin	80.9 KB	
☐ Setup Log Files	8.77 KB	
☐ Temporary files	0 bytes	
☑ Thumbnails	4.00 MB	⌄

Total amount of disk space you gain: 6.26 MB

Description

Downloaded Program Files are ActiveX controls and Java applets downloaded automatically from the Internet when you view certain pages. They are temporarily stored in the Downloaded Program Files folder on your hard disk.

Clean up system files   View Files

How does Disk Cleanup work?

OK   Cancel

43

Chapter 19: Creating a shortcut for booting into Advanced Startup Options

You are now aware of how you can boot into advanced setup options with a Windows 10 computer. However, the procedure was long, meaning that it will take you some time to do this. It is possible for you to create a shortcut on the desktop which you can use to boot directly into this option. You will just have to click on this shortcut, and then your computer will restart, booting into advanced startup options.

This can be done as follows in Windows 10:

On the desktop of your computer, right click on an empty area. Choose "new" and then select "shortcut."

A window will pop up. Just type the location box which is targeted. This should be as follows:

%windir%\system32\shutdown.exe /r /o /f /t 00

Give the shortcut a name of choice. I have given mine the name "AdvancedOptions." Once you are done with the name, click on "finish," and you will be done.

You shortcut will be ready for use. You can choose it the way it is. However, some of you might prefer to add an icon to it. To do this, follow the following steps:

Click on the shortcut you have created, and then select "properties."

Click on "Change Icon" option.

A list of icons will be presented to you. Feel free to choose the icon of choice. You might also need to browser in the System32 folder for bootux.dll file so as to set an icon for your shortcut.

If you need to quickly access the shortcut, you can choose to either pin it to the taskbar, create a keyboard shortcut for it, or just add it to the quick launch.

Chapter 20: Creating a Password Reset USB Drive

With Windows 10, it is possible for you to set your USB drive so that it can work as an emergency password reset disk. This feature is good for those who encounter a problem while trying to remember the password for their computer. With the password reset USB drive, you can be able to reset the password for the local Windows account of your computer. It will also be possible for you to reset the password as many times as possible using this drive. However, note that the password for your Microsoft account will not be changed.

For you to set the password reset USB drive, you must be logged in to your account. If the password is already forgotten, then it will be impossible for you to create this. This explains why you should set this early enough, as you don't know when you will forget your password.

To set a password rest the USB drive in Windows 10, and follow the steps below:

Sign in to the local OS account for which you want to create a password reset USB drive.

Open the control panel of the computer in small icons mode. Click on "User Accounts."

You can then connect the USB drive that you want to set as the password reset drive.

Look at the left side, and you will see an option labeled "create a password reset disk." Click on this option.

A wizard labeled "forgotten Password Wizard" will appear. Click on the "Next" button.

A list showing the available drives will be shown. Click on the one of choice. You can then click on the button labeled "Next."

You will be prompted to provide the password for your local account OS account. Just do that, and then click on "Next" button so as to proceed.

In case the USB drive already has the file "userkey.psw" in the root directory, you will be asked whether to overwrite it or not. Just overwrite it. If the file is not present, then this will not be the case.

This will have been set and then ready to use. If you need to setup another drive for this purpose, you just need to move the "userkey.psw" file to its root directory.

Chapter 21: Turning Cortana "on" or "off"

Cortana was introduced by Microsoft in Windows 10. It is an intelligent app for personal assistance. With Cortana, you can search in your Windows for files, apps, and settings. It is also possible to search in the web using Cortana.

What it does is that it learns from your activity and browsing history, and then it will be able to bring you reminders and any other relevant information. It is a very essential feature in Windows 10.

However, for Cortana to work in your computer, you have to set to the correct state. Just propagate to the Cortana window and then and on the upper left corner, click on the "Settings" icon.

The following procedure explains how you can manage Cortana settings:

Open "settings." Click on the "Privacy" icon.

A window will appear. Look at the options on the left window. Click on the "Speech, inking, & typing" option.

You should now turn on Cortana. Just click on "Get to know me."

If you need to turn it off, just click on "Stop getting to know me."

You are then done.

Chapter 22: Enabling Jump Lists in Start Menu

There are some components which you access on a frequent basis in your computer. These can be songs, documents, websites, or pictures. With jump lists, you can directly jump to these. However, if you are running it on Windows 10, then it will only work on elements which have been pinned to the task bar. However, you will not find this feature once you click on the start menu.

If you need to open this feature on an app which has already been pinned on the task bar, just right click on the button of the app. If you need to enable this feature for apps which are on the start menu, you will have to do some Registry tweaking as directed in the procedure below:

Click on Window + R. On the dialog that will appear, just type "regedit.exe."
Navigate to the following directory:
HKEY_CURRENT_USER\Software\Microsoft\Wind ows\CurrentVersion\Explorer\Advanced
Make a new Dword value, that is, 32 bit.
Give it the name "EnableJumpView."
Set the value of this to 1.
You can then restart your computer.

However, this procedure should be done with much care. In case something goes wrong, then the installation of your Windows might be negatively affected, and this effect can be permanent.

23: Enabling or Disabling Disk write protection

With the Microsoft Diskpart feature, it is possible for you to either enable or disable write protection on any of your computer hard drives in Windows 10. However, this feature is also supported in other versions of Windows such as Windows 7, Windows 8, and Windows Vista.

When a disk is write protected, other users will be unable to intentionally or accidentally delete data from it. This is a good practice for protection of your data. It is also an indication that you can't be able to use the disk in any meaningful way.

Open the command prompt. Make sure that you have opened it with administrative privileges. This can be done by right-clicking it and then choosing "Run as administrative." If prompted to allow the program to make changes to your computer, just select "Yes."

On the command prompt, just type "diskpart," and then press the "Enter" key.

On the same prompt, type "list disk," and then press the "Enter" key again.

Each disk will have a number next to it. Note the number associated with the disk on which you want to enable write protection.

Once you have noted the number, type the following on the command prompt: "select disk *", where "*" stands for the number which you noted in the previous step.

```
DISKPART> select disk 0
Disk 0 is now the selected disk.
DISKPART> attributes disk set readonly
```

We now need to enable write protection on the disk. Just type "attributes disk set readonly."

If you need to reverse this by removing the write protection on the disk, just type "attributes disk clear readonly."

You will be done. However, you need to know that it is impossible for us to write protect a Windows drive.

Chapter 24: Network and Internet

Windows 10 made it simple for the users to configure Internet settings. The steps for configuring a network and sharing have been made easy and few. The Homegroup feature has also been advanced.

To configure these settings, you have to go to the control panel just as in the previous versions of the Windows OS. However, the window for Network & Internet has more options for configuring connectivity on the right side of the window.

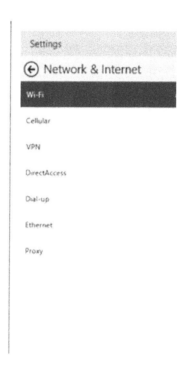

As shown in the above window, there are options for Cellular, Ethernet, VPN, Wi-Fi, DirectAccess, Dial-up, and Proxy. These are options that you expect when connecting either mobile or computer devices to a network or the Internet. These settings can also be used either at work or even at home.

You can use this window to set your proxy settings, Ethernet connections, wireless devices to be connected to your device, as well as the connections for the computer itself. However, a network card must be installed in your computer.

If you need to connect to your workplace environment, then it is possible for you to set up your VPN (Virtual Private Network) connection. This will let help you in the connection.

When navigating through the panel, all the available wireless connections will be shown. This means that you will be in a position to see all the computers, content, and devices which are available on the network. Devices such as printers which can be connected via the network are available here. Networks which are active have got properties.

These include the SSID (network name), the IP address, the protocol being used, and others. These can also be found in this section. The manufacturer of the network card being used, as well as its model can be known.

Chapter 25: Changing the number of Recent Items Displayed in Jump Lists

We discussed jump lists in our previous chapters, and we said that they enable us to jump to certain directories such as documents, pictures, music, and others. These are items which you frequently access on your computer.

Note that each application has a set of items which should appear in jump lists. An example is on notepad, which shows the .txt files which were recently opened with it. Google Chrome will also show a list of websites which have been recently accessed.

Note that in each of the applications used on your computer, jump list will show the 10 previously accessed items unless you set it to the number that you need. This is what we are going to discuss in this chapter.

Using Registry edit, this can be done as follows:

On your keyboard, just press the Windows + R keys. A dialog will appear. In it, type "regedit" and then press the "Enter" key on your keyboard.

Navigate to the following directory:

HKEY_CURRENT_USER\Software\Microsoft\Wind
ows\CurrentVersion\Explorer\Advanced

Once you are there, look at the window on the right
and click "Start_JumpListItems." We need to modify
it.
Provide a number which is in the range of 0 to 60.
After the above procedure, just restart your
computer.

Alternatively, the same result can be achieved with
the following procedure:

Open the control panel of your computer and then
click on "Taskbar and Navigation." Make sure that
you open it in the icons view mode.

Click on the tab labeled "Start Menu." You will see an
option labeled "Number of recent items to display in
Jump Lists." Change the value corresponding to this
to any number between 0 and 60.

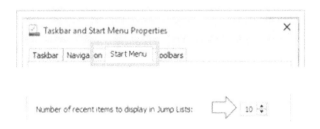

Click on the button labeled "Ok" so as to continue.

Chapter 26: Turning Aero Snap on or off

Aero Snap was introduced in Windows 7, and it is part of the enhancements made in Aero. With this feature, you can snap and resize open windows for comparing or working on them side-by-side.

If you need to snap a window, you just have to drag it to the edge of the screen, and a transparent overlay will be seen. The window can then be dropped so as to snap to the half of the screen. You can repeat the above procedure using another window, but drag it to the other edge of the screen. The two will then form a side by side window.

The Aero Snap can be turned on or off using the Settings app as explained below:
On your computer, open "Settings," and then choose the "System" icon.
A window will then appear. On the left side, look for "Multitasking," and then click on it.

You now need to turn Aero Snap on. On the right window labeled "Snap," move the slider right and next to "Allow the system to automatically arrange windows when they're moved to the corner or edge of the screen."

Underneath, you will find two Aero Snap settings. To turn them on, you just have to drag the slider which is next to them to the right.

If you need to turn Aero Snap off, look for the option labeled "Allow the system to automatically arrange windows when they're moved to the corner or edge of the screen" under the window labeled "Snap." Identify a slider which is next to it, and then move it to the left side. It will be off.

It is possible to turn this feature either on or off in the Ease of Access Center. This can be done as follows:

Open the control panel in the icons view mode. Choose "Ease of Access Center."
Once this has opened, you can chose among the following settings:
Make the mouse easier to use.
Make the keyboard easier to use.
Make it easier to focus on tasks.

These are shown in the following figure:

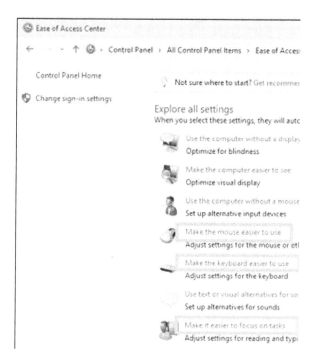

If you need to turn the Aero Snap on, then look for the checkbox next to the option labeled "Prevent windows from being automatically arranged when moved to the edge of the screen box," and then uncheck it.

If you need to turn the Aero Snap off, then identify the checkbox next to the option labeled "Prevent windows from being automatically arranged when moved to the edge of the screen box" and then check it.

Chapter 27: Unblocking a File

Windows 10 provides security to files contained in one's computer. This will prevent users of the system from running either unknown or unauthorized files. This protection is done using either SmartScreen or Open File. Whenever you try to open or access these files, then these will warn you. You will then be in a position to open those files which you can trust.

To open a file which has been blocked using Open File, follow the procedure below:

Open the file which has been blocked or the unknown one. The "Open File – Security Warning" prompt will be triggered.

The warning box will contain a checkbox labeled, "Always ask before opening this file." Uncheck this checkbox. You can then Run or Open the file.

In case you are prompted by UAC, just click on "yes" if you are logged in as the administrator or provide the administrator password.

If the file or application had been blocked using SmartScreen, you can unblock it via the following procedure:

Open the file which is blocked or unknown. The "Windows SmartScreen" warning prompt will be triggered.

Click on the link labeled "More Info."

You can then run the application by clicking on the button labeled "Run anyway." If you choose the button labeled "Don't run," the application or file will not be opened.

The file can also be unblocked in File properties as follows:

Move to the directory where the blocked file is stored, and right click on the file. Select "properties."

Click on the tap labeled "general." Identify a checkbox labeled "Block" at the bottom, and then check it.

A prompt can also appear. If it happens, just click on "continue."

If you are logged in as the administrator, a prompt will appear. Just click on "Yes" to continue. If you are logged in as a normal user, just provide the administrator password. If you cannot satisfy these conditions, then the app will not run or the file will not open.

Chapter 28: Rebuilding Icon Cache

All icons used for your files in the computer are stored in the icon cache. When displaying the files, the icon cache is then used for displaying the icons. This process has been made faster due to the use of the cache. Note that the icons are not stored in the memory of the computer, but in the cache. Whenever the file is opened, the icons are called from the cache rather than the memory.

Sometimes, you experience some problems with an icon when opening the file. This happens as a result of updating the application. If you fail to specify the new icon for the application, then it will show the old icon, and this can lead to a problem.

To build an icon cache, follow the steps below:

On your keyboard, press the Windows + R keys. A dialog will appear. Type "cmd" and then press the "enter" key.
Once the command prompt has opened, execute the following commands, but one at a time:
ie4uinit.exe –ClearIconCache
taskkill /IM explorer.exe /F
DEL "%localappdata%\IconCache.db" /A
shutdown /r /f /t oo

Before running the last command shown above, you need to have saved your important data as the command will restart the computer.

It is also possible for you to use File Explorer so as to delete the "IconCache.db" file. This can be done as follows:

Begin by opening File Explorer.
Click on the "View" tab, and then check the "Hidden Items" checkbox. This will show all the files which are hidden.

Navigate to the "C:\Users\(Your computer Name)\AppData\Local" directory. Find the file "IconCache.db" and then delete it.

Once done, empty the Recycle bin. Restart the computer.

Note that in case you already removed or deleted the icon file for this application, then the steps will not work.

Conclusion

It can be concluded that Windows 10 brought about numerous changes in the history of the Windows operating system. The operating system comes in various versions, and it can run on both PCs and mobile devices. The OS was developed so as to fill the gaps which were identified after the release of Windows 8 in the market. The OS will be run as a cloud, in which the components making it will be updated on a frequent basis.

Users of this OS will then be using the latest release of the OS. Once the OS has been released officially to the market, owners of Windows 7, Windows 8, and Windows 8.1 will be lucky as they upgrade to this new OS for free. A server version of the OS will also be released, and it will be used on production environments for security purposes.

After booting up the system running Windows 10, you will not be directly presented with the login screen. To access this, you will have to click on the Windows or press the "Enter" key. You will also notice a variety of options on this window, such as those for shutting down the system, restarting the system, and connecting to the Internet.

You can use these for those purposes. Once you have provided the password, just click on the arrow with the "->" symbol, or press the "Enter" key. This will take you to the home screen of the system if the password is correct. However, if the password is wrong, you will remain on the login screen. At the home screen, you will find numerous items pinned on the taskbar for easy and quick access.

www.ingramcontent.com/pod-product-compliance
Lightning Source LLC
Chambersburg PA
CBHW070855070326
40690CB00009B/1850

www.ingramcontent.com/pod-product-compliance
Lightning Source LLC
Chambersburg PA
CBHW070855070326
40690CB00009B/1850